sweet Revolution
COOKING WITHOUT SUGAR

DELICIOUS & HEALTHY RECIPES

by Chef Ozzie

Sweet Revolution
COOKING WITHOUT SUGAR

Published by Heartland Sweeteners

Copyright © 2010 by Heartland Sweeteners
14300 Clay Terrace Blvd.
Carmel, Indiana 46032

Photographer: Don Distel Photography
Food Stylist: Allison Douglass
Art Director: Shawn M. Hendrix
Editor: Jenny Thomas

Photograph page 6
© by Getty, Antonios Mitsopoulos
Photograph page 7 © by Purestock
Cover, chapter openers and food photography
© by Heartland Sweeteners, Don Distel

Library of Congress Control Number: 2010907766
ISBN: 978-0-9827629-0-5

Produced by

||| Favorite Recipes® Press

An imprint of

FRP.INC

a wholly owned subsidiary of
Southwestern/Great American, Inc.
P. O. Box 305142
Nashville, Tennessee 37230
800-358-0560

Manufactured in the United States of America
First Printing: 2010
15,000 copies

Hi, I'm Chef Ozzie! I've been cooking and baking since I was a child and have been in professional food service for over 30 years. I've always loved to cook, and when I discovered Ideal® No Calorie Sweetener, I was thrilled. Ideal® works great in all types of recipes and has allowed me to create, without sugar, the healthy and delicious treats in this cookbook. Enjoy and Bon Appétit!

Table of
Contents

Best Taste + Better Health...

For the most part, health and great taste are not two things that generally go together. How many times have you heard, "Everything that tastes good is bad for you, and everything that tastes bad is good for you?" In most cases this is true, but fortunately, not anymore. Chef Ozzie and Ideal® have teamed up to give everyone what they've been missing—health and great taste together. With the first no calorie sweetener that is preferred over sugar,* you can have your cake and eat it too!

*Preferred for sweetness vs. sugar in independent university taste tests.

Product Descriptions

Ideal® has many product options, providing a complete baking and cooking solution for a no-sugar-added diet!

Granular – No calorie sugar alternative for baking!

Packet – No calorie sugar alternative for sprinkling into beverages or on cereal!

Brown – No calorie brown sweetener for uses in many different recipes!

Confectionery – Low calorie powdered sweetener for frostings and sprinkling!

Ideal® Tips

Ideal® is the no calorie sweetener that people say they like better than sugar, and it's easy to use since it measures cup for cup just like sugar. The main ingredient in Ideal® is xylitol, which bakes a little differently than sugar in some recipes. These differences are listed below to help you get the best results possible.

✓ Cookies made with Ideal® may seem a bit drier than those made with sugar, and they may be a bit "puffier," but the taste is delicious compared to those made with sugar. Flatten the dough before baking to help cookies achieve the desired shape.

✓ Since xylitol does not feed yeast like sugar does, Ideal® is not suitable in breads that require yeast to rise. It does make delicious low-calorie quick breads and muffins, like Banana Bread and Raspberry Lemon Muffins.

✓ Xylitol doesn't brown like sugar, so adding honey, brown sugar, or molasses to a recipe will help achieve the desired browning. You can also spray the top of baked goods with a cooking spray during the last 10 minutes of baking.

✓ Baked goods made with Ideal® may bake more quickly than those made with sugar. Try reducing the time by 3 to 5 minutes for cookies and 5 to 8 minutes for cakes/muffins.

✓ To make sugar-free jams and jellies with Ideal®, be sure to use the "no-sugar-added" pectin designed specifically for sugar-free preserves. This will ensure proper gelling when you follow the directions on the package.

Baking Tips

The **"big three"** (**butter, milk and eggs**) work together in baking to achieve desired results. Altering any one in recipes or incorrect substitutions of any will result in a less desirable finished product. Solid fats add different qualities to a recipe than liquid fats, like oils. When creamed with a crystalline sweetener, butter creates and traps air and moisture in batter. While healthy oils are good for adding moisture, they cannot aerate, melt, or provide flakiness like solid fats do. This means you can use healthy margarines for fat in some recipes, but sometimes small amounts of butter are required for that taste difference.

When using **butter** substitutes, avoid solid or tub spreads that are less than 65% vegetable oil, as these contain too much water and will not result in a quality baked product. Light butter is good for the flavor profile but contains high levels of water.

In low-fat baking the flavorings must be increased to compensate for the reduction in butter.

Fat Chart (per 1 TBS)

Source	Calories	Total Fat	Saturated Fat	Trans Fat	Monosaturated Fat	Cholesterol
Corn Oil	120	14	2	0	4	0
Canola Oil	120	14	1	0	8	0
Butter	102	11.5	7.2	0	3	31
Margarine	100	11	2	2.5	5.5	0
Margarine 70%	90	10	2	2	4	0
Smart Balance® Stick	100	11	5	0	3.5	15
Smart Balance® Spread	80	9	2.5	0	3.5	0

Keep these tips in mind for best results: Use reduced fat (vs. totally fat-free) items to enable better creaming to make cakes light and fluffy. With no fat, baked goods become dense and texture is significantly altered.

Mix fats and flour together only until combined (or follow directions) to avoid a tough finished product.

*Smart Balance® is a registered trademark of GFA Brands, Inc.

Shortenings... (butter, margarine, vegetable shortening) coat flour proteins and "shorten" the length of their gluten strands when mixed with moisture, hence "shortenings."

Vegetable oils do not act as a shortener as they won't cream with crystalline sweeteners.

In low-fat baking, never bake two trays of cookies simultaneously as heat will not distribute evenly.

Milk Comparisons

	Whole	Skim
Calories	150	80
Fat	8g	0g
Sat Fat	5g	0g
Sugars	11g	12g
Cholesterol	35mg	<5mg

Milk...

Buttermilk is used frequently in low-fat baking to help tenderize. This is very important in recipes low in sugar and fats. Homemade buttermilk can be made by adding one tablespoon of vinegar or lemon juice to one cup of 1% (low-fat) milk; allow to stand for several minutes before using.

Eggs...

Warm eggs hold more air and create more volume when they are whipped than cold eggs do.

Whipping egg whites separately from egg yolks adds even more volume to a sponge cake batter.

To use ½ of a whole egg in a recipe, beat egg and then measure 2 tablespoons into the recipe. One large egg equals 4 tablespoons.

1 Cup of Eggs=

Size	Whole	Whites	Yolks
Jumbo	4	5	11
X-Large	4	6	12
Large	4	9	13
Medium	5	8	16
Small	6	9	18

Beating egg whites at room temperature is very important. The proteins in the whites expand better when warm, so you will get better volume from the eggs. Older eggs also whip more easily because of chemical changes that have taken place as they aged.

How can you tell when the whites are done? Place an uncooked egg (thoroughly cleaned) on top of the foam. If it sinks ¼ inch into the foam, your whites are perfect. If it doesn't sink at all, you've gone too far.

Testimonials

" Thank you so much for your product! I have tried it and compared it against other sweeteners; hands down, Ideal® No Calorie Sweetener is by far the best no calorie sweetener choice! I don't know why anyone wouldn't use this product in place of sugar. "

J. Griffith, Delaware

" I just want to say that I think Ideal® Sweetener is fantastic. I made cake with it, and when I tasted the batter, I noticed absolutely no aftertaste!!! Then when we tasted the finished product...no aftertaste!! So, this morning, I decided to try Ideal® in a cup of hot tea. It tasted just like sugar!!! I was soooo happy because in the winter, I love hot tea. Thank you for a fantastic product!!! "

Cheryl, Colorado

" I am so glad I found your sweetener. I love baking with it. The Cinnamon Cookies were the first item I baked. Boy, were they a hit at my house. They taste just like snickerdoodle cookies. The next thing I made was a Strawberry Cream Pie using your Coconut Cream Pie recipe. It was out of this world!!!! I can hardly wait to try the Pumpkin Bread and the Chocolate Cookies. I have also incorporated it into some of my recipes like chocolate oatmeal no-bake cookies. Again, thanks for a great product. Every time I see someone purchasing another no calorie sweetener, I tell them about Ideal®. "

Rebecca, North Carolina

" I just wanted to let you know that I really enjoy baking with your product. This year we celebrated Chinese New Year 'The Year of the Tiger,' and dessert is especially important. I made the sugar-free cheesecake recipe and no-one could tell that it was sugar-free. I was elated at how it turned out. I will be telling all my friends and customers about it. "

Margaret, California

Sweet
Tooth

No-Dairy Chocolate Cake

Serves: 12

Ingredients

3 cups all-purpose flour

$2/3$ cup unsweetened cocoa powder

2 teaspoons baking soda

2 cups Ideal® No Calorie Sweetener

1 teaspoon salt

6 tablespoons canola oil

4 tablespoons olive oil

3 teaspoons pure vanilla extract

2 tablespoons cider vinegar

2 cups cold water

Directions

1. Preheat oven to 350°F.
2. Grease and flour two 8-inch round cake pans.
3. Sift and mix together flour, cocoa, baking soda, Ideal® and salt.
4. In a separate bowl, whisk together oils, vanilla, vinegar and water.
5. Whisk in dry ingredients and blend until completely free of lumps.
6. Pour into prepared pans and bake for 20 to 25 minutes or until top springs back when pressed gently.
7. Cool before removing from pans.
8. Frost with Ideal® Chocolate or Buttercream Frosting.

Per Serving: 270 Calories, 4g Protein, 12g Total Fat, 35g Carbohydrates, 2g Fiber, 0g Sugar, 410mg Sodium, 0mg Cholesterol

One serving of dark chocolate has more antioxidants than a serving of blueberries or cranberries.

Chef Ozzie Tips

1 square chocolate = 4 tablespoons cocoa and $1/2$ tablespoon fat; 1 pound grated chocolate = about $3^1/2$ cups

Decadent Chocolate Torte

Serves: 12

Ingredients

CAKE

12 ounces (1$\frac{1}{2}$ cups) sugar-
free chocolate, chopped
$\frac{3}{4}$ cup (1$\frac{1}{2}$ sticks) unsalted
butter, cut into pieces

6 large eggs, separated
12 tablespoons Ideal®
No Calorie Sweetener
2 teaspoons vanilla extract

GANACHE

1 cup sugar-free
whipping cream
9 ounces (1$\frac{1}{8}$ cups) sugar-free
chocolate, chopped
Chocolate shavings

Top with Ideal®
Whipped Cream or
Ideal® Vanilla Bean
Ice Cream.

Directions

FOR CAKE:

1. Preheat oven to 350°F. Butter a 9-inch diameter springform pan. Line bottom of pan with parchment or waxed paper; butter paper. Wrap outside of pan with foil.
2. Stir chocolate and butter in heavy medium saucepan over low heat until melted and smooth. Remove from heat. Cool to lukewarm, stirring often.
3. Using an electric mixer, beat egg yolks and 6 tablespoons of Ideal® in a large bowl until thick and pale yellow (about 3 minutes). Fold lukewarm chocolate mixture into yolk mixture, and then fold in vanilla extract.
4. Using clean, dry beaters, beat egg whites in another bowl until soft peaks form. Gradually add remaining 6 tablespoons of Ideal®, beating until stiff peaks form. Fold whites into chocolate mixture in three additions. Pour batter into prepared pan.
5. Bake cake until top is puffed and cracking and tester inserted into center comes out with some moist crumbs attached (about 50 minutes). Cool cake in pan on rack (cake will fall).

6. Gently press down cracked top to make an even cake. Using a small knife, cut around pan side to loosen cake. Remove pan side. Place a 9-inch tart pan bottom or cardboard round on top of cake. Invert cake onto bottom and remove parchment/waxed paper.

For Ganache:

1. Bring cream to a boil and remove from heat just when it is about to boil over. Add chocolate and whisk until melted and smooth.
2. Place cake on rack over baking sheet. Spread $1/2$ cup of ganache over top and side of cake. Freeze until almost set (about 4 minutes).
3. Pour remaining ganache over cake; smooth top and side. Place cake on platter; chill until firm. Garnish with chocolate shavings and serve. Serve at room temperature.

Per Serving: 400 Calories, 3g Protein, 29g Total Fat, 35g Carbohydrates, 3g Fiber, 1g Sugar, 35mg Sodium, 140mg Cholesterol

Angel Food Cake

Serves: 16

Ingredients

¾ cup Ideal® No Calorie Sweetener

1 cup sifted cake flour

1½ cups egg whites (10 to 12 large),
  room temperature

1 teaspoon cream of tartar

¼ teaspoon salt

¾ cup Ideal® No Calorie Sweetener

2 teaspoons pure vanilla extract

½ teaspoon almond extract

Directions

1. Preheat oven to 325°F.
2. In a small bowl, whisk together ¾ cup of Ideal® and cake flour. Set aside.
3. Beat egg whites until frothy; add cream of tartar and salt. Beat until fully incorporated, then begin to add the remaining ¾ cup of Ideal® 1 to 2 tablespoons at a time. Beat egg white mixture to soft peaks. Slow mixer down if needed to assure you do not overbeat. Do not beat to stiff peaks.
4. Add vanilla and almond extracts and beat only until evenly distributed.
5. Sift Ideal® and cake flour mixture over the egg whites in 6 to 8 additions and gently fold it in after each addition. Take your time with this step as not to overfold and deflate the egg whites.
6. Spoon batter into an ungreased tube pan with removable bottom or an angel food cake pan. Smooth top with a spatula and tap gently on the counter once or twice to ensure that there are no large air pockets.
7. Bake for 40 to 50 minutes, until the top springs back when lightly pressed.
8. Remove cake from oven and invert on a bottle. Allow to cool completely or overnight.

Chef Ozzie Tips

You will know when you have soft peaks because the egg whites will look like soft waves and when you lift the beaters,

9. Gently run thin knife around the sides, then around the bottom of the pan to release the cake.

Per Serving: 60 Calories, 3g Protein, 0g Total Fat, 10g Carbohydrates, 0g Fiber, 0g Sugar, 75mg Sodium, 0mg Cholesterol

Chef Ozzie Tips

the peaks will droop back down into the batter. If your batter is falling in ribbon-like patterns, it is not quite there.

Carrot Cake

Serves: 12

Ingredients

2 cups white whole
   wheat flour
2 teaspoons baking soda
1/2 teaspoon salt
2 1/2 teaspoons cinnamon

3/4 cup egg substitute
2 cups Ideal® No Calorie
   Sweetener
3/4 cup vegetable oil
3/4 cup buttermilk
2 teaspoons vanilla extract

2 cups grated carrot
1 (8-ounce) can crushed
   pineapple, drained
1 cup toasted coconut
1 cup chopped pecans
   or walnuts

Directions

1. Preheat oven to 350°F.
2. Line 2 (9-inch) round cake pans with waxed paper; lightly grease and flour waxed paper. Set pans aside.
3. Stir together flour, baking soda, salt, and cinnamon.
4. Beat egg substitute, Ideal®, oil, buttermilk, and vanilla at medium speed with an electric mixer until smooth. Add flour mixture, beating at low speed until blended. Fold in carrot, pineapple, coconut and chopped nuts. Pour batter into prepared cake pans.
5. Bake for 25 to 30 minutes or until a wooden pick inserted in center comes out clean. Cool in pans on wire racks for 15 minutes. Remove from pans and cool completely on wire racks.

Per Serving: 380 Calories, 7g Protein, 25g Total Fat, 34g Carbohydrates, 5g Fiber, 7g Sugar, 370mg Sodium, 0mg Cholesterol

Chef Ozzie Tips

Spread Ideal® Cream Cheese Frosting between layers and on top and side of cake.

Yellow Cake

Serves: 12

Ingredients

½ cup (1 stick) unsalted butter, softened
1 cup Ideal® No Calorie Sweetener
2 eggs
1½ cups sifted cake flour

1½ teaspoons baking powder
¼ teaspoon salt
½ cup milk
½ teaspoon pure vanilla extract
¼ teaspoon almond extract

Directions

1. Preheat oven to 350°F.
2. Grease and flour a 9-inch cake pan.
3. Cream butter and slowly add Ideal®, creaming until light and fluffy.
4. Add eggs one at a time, beating after each addition.
5. In a separate bowl, sift flour with baking powder and salt.
6. Add flour mixture alternating with milk, vanilla and almond extracts to creamed mixture, beating after each addition until smooth.
7. Pour batter into cake pan.
8. Bake 20 to 25 minutes or until toothpick inserted in center comes out clean.
9. Cool cake in pan 10 minutes and then remove to rack to finish cooling.

Per Serving: 150 Calories, 3g Protein, 9g Total Fat, 16g Carbohydrates, 0g Fiber, 1g Sugar, 135mg Sodium, 55mg Cholesterol

Chef Ozzie Tips

Frost with Ideal®
Chocolate
Buttercream Frosting.

Buttercream Frosting

Serves: 24

Ingredients

6 tablespoons (¾ stick) unsalted
butter, softened

2 cups Ideal® Confectionery Sweetener
3 tablespoons fat-free milk
1 teaspoon pure vanilla extract

Directions

1. Beat butter in medium bowl until creamy.
2. Add Ideal® Confectionery gradually into creamed butter alternating with milk until frosting reaches desired consistency for spreading.
3. Stir in vanilla extract.

VARIATIONS:

Mocha: add ½ teaspoon coffee extract with the vanilla

Chocolate: combine ½ cup unsweetened cocoa powder with Ideal® Confectionery plus 2 tablespoons hot water

Lemon: replace milk with fresh lemon juice and 1 teaspoon lemon zest, minced fine

Orange: replace milk with fresh orange juice and 1 teaspoon orange zest, minced fine

Sour Cream: add 3 tablespoons sour cream with the butter and beat until creamy

Per Serving: 60 Calories, 0g Protein, 3g Total Fat, 7g Carbohydrates, 0g Fiber, 0g Sugar, 10mg Sodium, 10mg Cholesterol

Chef Ozzie Tips

During warmer and humid seasons, replace 3 tablespoons butter with 3 tablespoons solid vegetable shortening.

Cream Cheese Frosting

Serves: 24

Ingredients

2 (8-ounce) packages cream cheese, softened
½ cup (1 stick) unsalted butter, softened

1 teaspoon pure vanilla extract
2 cups sifted Ideal® Confectionery Sweetener

Directions

1. In a medium bowl, cream together cream cheese and butter until smooth.
2. Mix in the vanilla, then gradually add Ideal® Confectionery and mix until smooth.
3. Store in refrigerator.

Per Serving: 130 Calories, 1g Protein, 10g Total Fat, 8g Carbohydrates, 0g Fiber, 1g Sugar, 70mg Sodium, 30mg Cholesterol

Chef Ozzie Tips

Microwave unwrapped cream cheese at 50% power for 20 seconds to soften.

In Pennsylvania, New Jersey, the Lower Midwest, and the entire South, the preferred term is "icing."

Coconut Cream Pie

Serves: 8

Ingredients

1¼ cups Ideal® No Calorie Sweetener

½ cup all-purpose flour

¼ teaspoon salt

3 cups milk

4 egg yolks

3 tablespoons butter

¾ cup unsweetened flaked
coconut, toasted

1 teaspoon pure vanilla extract

½ teaspoon coconut extract

1 (9-inch) pie shell, baked

Directions

1. In medium saucepan, combine Ideal®, flour and salt over medium heat; gradually add milk and cook until the mixture is thick and bubbly.
2. Temper yolks by adding ½ cup scalded milk mixture to yolks and whisk well. Add yolk mixture back into milk mixture; whisk vigorously over medium heat until thickened (about 2 minutes).
3. Reduce heat to low and cook 2 more minutes; remove from heat.
4. Stir in butter, flaked coconut, vanilla and coconut extract; pour filling into prebaked pie shell; cool.
5. Cover and chill if not serving immediately; store leftovers in refrigerator.

Per Serving: 340 Calories, 7g Protein, 19g Total Fat, 35g Carbohydrates, 2g Fiber, 5g Sugar, 240mg Sodium, 115mg Cholesterol

Chef Ozzie Tips

Can be topped with Ideal® Whipped Cream and additional toasted coconut.

Ozzie's Chocolate Coconut Dream

Serves: 8

Ingredients

HAUPIA:

1 (13.5-ounce) can coconut milk
1 cup milk
1 cup Ideal® No Calorie Sweetener
$1/2$ cup cornstarch
1 cup water

ASSEMBLY:

7 ounces semi-sweet chocolate
$1/2$ teaspoon coconut extract
1 (9-inch) pie shell, baked
$1^{1}/_{2}$ cups heavy whipping cream
$1/4$ cup Ideal® No Calorie Sweetener

Chef Ozzie Tips

Never add cornstarch or flour directly to a recipe to thicken. Always dissolve in water, milk, or broth before incorporating into the recipe.

Directions

1. Whisk together coconut milk, milk and 1 cup Ideal® in a small saucepan. In separate bowl, dissolve cornstarch in water. Bring coconut milk mixture to a boil, then reduce to a simmer and whisk in cornstarch mixture until thickened.
2. Microwave chocolate pieces on High 1 minute; stir to melt completely. Pour half of haupia mixture into a bowl and mix in coconut extract. Mix remaining haupia with melted chocolate and pour over bottom of baked pie crust. Layer white haupia over top; cool pie at least 1 hour in refrigerator.
3. Whip cream with $1/4$ cup Ideal® until stiff peaks form. Garnish pie with whipped topping, toasted coconut and shaved chocolate, chill an additional hour and serve.

Per Serving: 580 Calories, 6g Protein, 42g Total Fat, 50g Carbohydrates, 2g Fiber, 16g Sugar, 160mg Sodium, 65mg Cholesterol

Apple Pie
Serves: 8

Ingredients

CRUST:
2 cups all-purpose flour
$1/2$ teaspoon salt
$1/2$ cup (1 stick) unsalted butter
$1/2$ cup ice water
or: 1 unbaked double
   pie pastry

FILLING:
7 cups baking apples
   (Granny Smith), sliced thin,
   cored, peeled
1 teaspoon pure vanilla extract
1 cup Ideal® No Calorie
   Sweetener

3 tablespoons
   all-purpose flour
1 teaspoon cornstarch
3 teaspoons ground
   cinnamon
$1/8$ teaspoon salt
1 egg yolk
1 tablespoon water

Directions

1. In a large bowl, combine flour and salt. Cut in butter until mixture resembles coarse crumbs and begin stirring in water one tablespoon at a time until a ball is formed. Divide dough into two portions and shape into balls. Wrap in plastic and refrigerate for 4 hours or overnight. Roll one ball out and fit into a 9-inch pie pan or dish.
2. Preheat oven to 425°F.
3. Place sliced apples into a large mixing bowl. Sprinkle with vanilla, toss and set aside. Combine Ideal®, flour, cornstarch, cinnamon and salt in small bowl. Sprinkle mixture over apples and toss. Allow mix to weep out moisture for 10 minutes. Spoon apple mixture into pie crust. Place the second crust over the filling. Seal edges, trim and flute. Make small opening in top of crust for steam to escape during baking.

Chef Ozzie Tips

Cover outer crust with foil toward end of baking to prevent burning. Serve with Ideal® Vanilla Bean Ice Cream and Ideal® Whipped Cream.

4. Beat egg yolk and water; brush over pie (optional).

5. Bake for 20 minutes. Reduce temperature to 325°F and bake an additional 30 to 35 minutes or until the top crust is golden and filling is bubbling. Serve warm or chilled.

Per Serving: 310 Calories, 4g Protein, 13g Total Fat, 46g Carbohydrates, 4g Fiber, 10g Sugar, 190mg Sodium, 55mg Cholesterol

Blueberry Pie
Serves: 8

Ingredients

¾ cup Ideal® No Calorie Sweetener

3 tablespoons cornstarch

2 tablespoons lemon juice

1 tablespoon lemon zest

4 cups fresh blueberries

1 (9-inch) unbaked double pie pastry

Directions

1. Preheat oven to 400°F.
2. In a small bowl, mix Ideal®, cornstarch, lemon juice and zest. Place blueberries in a large bowl. Add the Ideal® mixture to the blueberries and gently toss to combine. Fit one of the pie pastries into a pie plate or dish. Pour the blueberry mixture into the pie pastry.
3. Starting on the outside edge, place top pastry on pie. Seal edges and pinch neatly to seal entire crust. Place pie in refrigerator for 30 minutes to chill.
4. Remove pie from refrigerator and place on baking sheet in preheated oven on the lower third rack.
5. Bake for 20 minutes and then reduce the oven temperature to 350°F. Continue baking for 35 to 40 minutes or until crust is deep golden brown and juices are bubbling and thick. Place pie on rack to cool for several hours. Serve at room temperature with Ideal® Whipped Cream or Ideal® Vanilla Bean Ice Cream.

Per Serving: 190 Calories, 2g Protein, 8g Total Fat, 29g Carbohydrates, 3g Fiber, 8g Sugar, 120mg Sodium, 0mg Cholesterol

Chef Ozzie Tips

Mix one large egg with one tablespoon cream and brush over pie for a golden brown crust.

Blueberries are naturally low in both fat and sodium.

Pumpkin Pie

Serves: 8

Ingredients

1 (8-ounce) package low-fat cream cheese

2 cups (one 15-ounce can) canned pumpkin, mashed (not pie filling)

1 cup Ideal® No Calorie Sweetener

¼ teaspoon salt

¼ cup egg substitute

2 egg yolks, slightly beaten

1 cup half & half

¼ cup (½ stick) margarine, melted

1½ teaspoons pure vanilla extract

½ teaspoon ground cinnamon

1 (9-inch) pie shell, baked

Directions

1. Preheat oven to 350°F.

2. In a large mixing bowl, beat the cream cheese with hand mixer until soft and creamy. Add the pumpkin and beat until combined. Add the Ideal® and salt until combined. Add egg substitute, egg yolks, half & half and melted margarine. Beat until combined and then add vanilla and cinnamon; mix well.

3. Pour filling into warm prepared pie crust and bake for 50 minutes or until center is set. Cover the crust with foil if needed to prevent overbrowning.

4. Place pie on rack to cool to room temperature.

Per Serving: 340 Calories, 7g Protein, 22g Total Fat, 29g Carbohydrates, 3g Fiber, 4g Sugar, 410mg Sodium, 80mg Cholesterol

Chef Ozzie Tips

Can be topped with Ideal® Whipped Cream.

New York Cheesecake

Serves: 16

Ingredients

1¼ cups graham cracker crumbs

¼ cup butter substitute spread

5 (8-ounce) packages cream cheese, softened

1 cup Ideal® No Calorie Sweetener

1 teaspoon lemon juice

3 tablespoons flour

1 tablespoon pure vanilla extract

1 cup light sour cream

1 cup egg substitute

Directions

1. Preheat oven to 325°F if using a silver 9-inch springform pan (or to 300°F if using a dark nonstick 9-inch springform pan). Mix crumbs and butter substitute; press firmly onto bottom of pan. Bake 10 minutes.

2. Beat cream cheese, Ideal®, lemon juice, flour and vanilla in large bowl with electric mixer on medium speed until well blended. Add sour cream; mix well. Add egg substitute, ¼ cup at a time, mixing on low speed after each addition just until blended. Pour over crust.

3. Bake 1 hour 10 minutes or until center is almost set. Run knife or metal spatula around rim of pan to loosen cake; cool before removing rim of pan. Refrigerate 4 hours or overnight. Store leftover cheesecake in refrigerator.

Per Serving: 340 Calories, 8g Protein, 29g Total Fat, 13g Carbohydrates, 0g Fiber, 6g Sugar, 330mg Sodium, 85mg Cholesterol

Chef Ozzie Tips

Top with your favorite fruit topping and Ideal® Whipped Cream.

Cinnamon Cookies

Serves: 32

Ingredients

1 cup Ideal® No Calorie Sweetener

¹/₂ cup (1 stick) unsalted butter, softened

1 large egg

1 teaspoon pure vanilla extract

1¹/₂ cups all-purpose flour

1¹/₂ teaspoons cinnamon

1 teaspoon baking powder

¹/₄ teaspoon salt

3 tablespoons Ideal® No Calorie Sweetener

2 teaspoons cinnamon

Directions

1. In a mixing bowl, cream together 1 cup Ideal® and butter; beat in egg and vanilla.
2. Sift together flour, 1¹/₂ teaspoons cinnamon, baking powder and salt. Add to butter mixture and blend well until ball is formed.
3. Cover and refrigerate 2 hours or until firm enough to roll into balls.
4. Shape dough into small balls about 1 inch in diameter.
5. Mix 3 tablespoons of Ideal® and 2 teaspoons cinnamon. Roll balls in mixture.
6. Set cookies on lightly greased cookie sheets and press down until ¹/₄ inch thick.
7. Bake at 350°F for 10 minutes or until edges are lightly browned.
8. Cool slightly on pans, then remove to racks to cool completely.

Per Serving: 60 Calories, 1g Protein, 3g Total Fat, 7g Carbohydrates, 0g Fiber, 0g Sugar, 40mg Sodium, 15mg Cholesterol

Chef Ozzie Tips

Cinnamon loses its flavor over time so it should be used within a year for optimal taste.

Studies have shown that just ½ teaspoon of cinnamon per day can lower LDL cholesterol. Several studies suggest that cinnamon may have a regulatory effect on blood sugar, making it especially beneficial for people with Type 2 diabetes.

Sugar Cookies

Serves: 32

Ingredients

1 cup Ideal® No Calorie Sweetener
½ cup (1 stick) unsalted butter, softened
1 large egg

1 teaspoon pure vanilla extract
1½ cups all-purpose flour
1 teaspoon baking powder
¼ teaspoon salt

Directions

1. In a mixing bowl, cream together Ideal® and butter; beat in egg and vanilla.
2. Sift together flour, baking powder and salt, and then add to butter mixture.
3. Blend well until ball is formed (may have to form by hand to gather all crumbs).
4. Cover dough and refrigerate 2 hours.
5. Temper dough until soft enough to roll.
6. Roll dough out between two pieces of parchment paper to ⅛ inch thickness.
7. Cut into desired shapes and set cookies on lightly greased cookie sheets.
8. Bake at 350°F for 8 to 10 minutes or until edges are lightly browned.
9. Cool slightly on pans, then remove to racks to cool completely.

Per Serving: 50 Calories, 1g Protein, 2g Total Fat, 6g Carbohydrates, 0g Fiber, 0g Sugar, 40mg Sodium, 10mg Cholesterol

If you bake in the humid heat of summer and your cookies spread too much or turn soggy, try adding 1 or 2 extra tablespoons of flour to the recipe. If your cookie dough mixture is dry, add an egg yolk instead of water.

Chef Ozzie Tips

A dusting of flour while rolling will reduce sticking. Sprinkle top of cookies with Ideal® before baking. Add ½ teaspoon lemon zest for a twist to this recipe.

Peanut Butter Cookies

Serves: 24

Ingredients

½ cup butter substitute spread, softened

½ cup Ideal® No Calorie Sweetener

½ cup Ideal® Brown Sweetener

¼ cup low-fat creamy peanut butter

¼ cup creamy peanut butter

¼ cup egg substitute

1¼ cups white whole wheat flour

¾ teaspoon baking soda

¼ teaspoon baking powder

¼ teaspoon salt

Directions

1. Preheat oven to 375°F.
2. Cream butter substitute for 2 minutes; add Ideal® sweeteners and cream for an additional 2 minutes. Mix in peanut butters and egg substitute.
3. Mix together the dry ingredients and stir into butter substitute mixture.
4. Wrap dough in plastic and refrigerate for at least 3 hours.
5. Shape/scoop dough into 1¼-inch balls and place 3 inches apart on ungreased cookie sheets. Flatten in crisscross pattern with fork dipped in flour. Bake for 7 to 9 minutes until light brown.

Per Serving: 90 Calories, 3g Protein, 6g Total Fat, 9g Carbohydrates, 1g Fiber, 3g Sugar, 135mg Sodium, 0mg Cholesterol

Chef Ozzie Tips

Best when eaten soon after removing from oven. If you want a gooier cookie, experiment with removing from oven between 5 and 8 minutes.

Raspberry-Filled Shortbread Cookies

Serves: 16

Ingredients

1 cup (2 sticks) unsalted butter, softened

2/3 cup Ideal® No Calorie Sweetener

1/2 teaspoon almond extract

2 cups all-purpose flour

1/3 cup sugar-free seedless raspberry jam

Directions

1. Preheat oven to 350°F.
2. In a medium bowl or mixer, cream butter and Ideal®; add almond extract.
3. Gradually add flour until dough forms a ball.
4. Remove, cover and refrigerate for 1 hour or until easy to handle.
5. Roll dough into 1-inch balls and place 1 inch apart on ungreased baking sheets.
6. Make indentation in center of cookie with handle of wooden spoon or similar and fill with jam.
7. Bake for 12 to 15 minutes.
8. Remove to wire racks and cool.
9. Spoon additional jam into cookies, if desired.

Per Serving: 170 Calories, 2g Protein, 12g Total Fat, 16g Carbohydrates, 0g Fiber, 0g Sugar, 0mg Sodium, 30mg Cholesterol

Chef Ozzie Tips

If you substitute salted butter for unsalted butter in a recipe, make sure you reduce the amount of salt called for in the recipe.

Salted butter contains 1 to 2 teaspoons of sodium per pound or 1/4 to 1/2 teaspoon per stick.

Double Chocolate Cookies

Serves: 24

Ingredients

2 cups all-purpose flour

1/2 teaspoon salt

1 teaspoon baking soda

1²/₃ cups Ideal® No Calorie Sweetener

1/3 cup unsweetened cocoa powder

1¼ cups (2½ sticks) light butter

2 large eggs

1 teaspoon pure vanilla extract

1 cup semisweet chocolate chips

Directions

1. Preheat oven to 350°F.
2. Combine flour, salt, baking soda, Ideal® and cocoa powder in a large bowl.
3. In separate bowl, beat butter until it is light and fluffy; add eggs and vanilla and beat until combined.
4. Add dry mixture to wet mixture and stir until well combined.
5. Fold in chocolate chips by hand.
6. Drop by spoonfuls onto greased or parchment paper-lined cookie sheets and bake for 10 to 12 minutes or until toothpick inserted comes out clean.

Per Serving: 170 Calories, 3g Protein, 10g Total Fat, 18g Carbohydrates, 1g Fiber, 5g Sugar, 110mg Sodium, 30mg Cholesterol

Chef Ozzie Tips

Use sugar-free chips for even further reduced sugar. Eliminate chips and make sandwich cookies with favorite frosting as filling for a special treat.

Oatmeal Raisin Cookies

Serves: 24

Ingredients

1¼ cups butter substitute, softened

½ cup Ideal® No Calorie Sweetener

1 cup Ideal® Brown Sweetener

½ cup egg substitute

2 teaspoons pure vanilla extract

1½ cups all-purpose flour

1 teaspoon baking soda

1½ teaspoons cinnamon

½ teaspoon salt

3 cups quick or whole old-fashioned oats

1 cup raisins

Directions

1. Preheat oven to 350°F.
2. Cream together butter substitute, Ideal® and Ideal® Brown.
3. Add egg substitute and vanilla; beat well.
4. Combine and sift flour, baking soda, cinnamon and salt; mix well into egg mixture.
5. Stir in oats and raisins and mix well.
6. Drop by spoonfuls onto ungreased cookie sheets; press slightly to flatten.
7. Bake 10 to 12 minutes or until golden in color; rotate cookie sheets for even cooking.

Per Serving: 180 Calories, 3g Protein, 9g Total Fat, 23g Carbohydrates, 2g Fiber, 4g Sugar, 180mg Sodium, 0mg Cholesterol

Chef Ozzie Tips

Make bar cookies by baking batter in an ungreased 9X13-inch baking dish. Add dried cranberries, cherries, or chocolate chips for more flavor. Store in airtight containers.

Vanilla Bean Ice Cream

Serves: 8

Ingredients

2 cups half & half

1 cup heavy whipping cream

1 cup Ideal® No Calorie Sweetener

1 vanilla bean, split lengthwise and seeds scraped

Directions

1. Combine all ingredients (including the bean and its pulp) in a large saucepan and place over medium heat. Attach a thermometer (candy or frying) to inside of pan.

2. Stirring occasionally, bring mixture to 170°F. Remove from heat and allow to cool slightly.

3. Remove the bean and pulp and discard; pour remaining mixture into lidded container and refrigerate overnight to allow flavors to mature.

4. Freeze mixture in ice cream freezer according to the manufacturer's instructions. The mixture will not freeze hard in machine. Once the volume has increased by $1/2$ to $3/4$ times its original volume and reached a soft consistency, spoon mixture back into lidded container. Add your favorite cookie, candy or flavoring for different treats. Top with Ideal® Whipped Cream. Harden in freezer for at least an hour before serving.

Per Serving: 210 Calories, 2g Protein, 18g Total Fat, 9g Carbohydrates, 0g Fiber, 0g Sugar, 35mg Sodium, 65mg Cholesterol

Chef Ozzie Tips

If not using thermometer, bring mixture just barely to a simmer. As soon as you see a bubble hit the surface, remove from heat. DO NOT BOIL.

Strawberry Sorbet

Serves: 6

Ingredients

2 cups water
1 cup Ideal® No Calorie Sweetener

1 quart fresh strawberries, hulled
1/3 cup fresh orange juice
1/3 cup fresh lemon juice

Directions

1. Stir water and Ideal® in medium saucepan over high heat until Ideal® dissolves. Boil for 5 minutes.

2. Purée strawberries in food processor until smooth. Add strawberry purée, orange juice and lemon juice to Ideal® syrup; stir to blend. Cover and refrigerate until cold (about 2 hours) or overnight.

3. Process strawberry mixture in ice cream maker per manufacturer's instructions or place in shallow container and freeze, stirring every hour until set (about 6 to 8 hours).

4. Cover and freeze in airtight container.

Per Serving: 70 Calories, 1g Protein, 0g Total Fat, 18g Carbohydrates, 2g Fiber, 6g Sugar, 0mg Sodium, 0mg Cholesterol

Chef Ozzie Tips

If too cold or frozen solid, place in refrigerator for 20 minutes to soften.

Chocolate Pudding

Serves: 8

Ingredients

¼ cup cornstarch
½ cup Ideal® No Calorie Sweetener
⅛ teaspoon salt

3 cups 2% milk
6 ounces (1 cup) sugar-free chocolate chips
1 teaspoon pure vanilla extract

Directions

1. Combine the cornstarch, Ideal® and salt in the top of a double boiler.
2. Slowly whisk in milk, scraping the bottom and side to incorporate all ingredients thoroughly. Stir constantly until mixture becomes thick enough to evenly coat a spoon (about 20 minutes).
3. When thickened, add chocolate and continue stirring 2 to 4 more minutes (until pudding is smooth).
4. Remove from heat and stir in vanilla.
5. Strain through a fine mesh strainer into a serving bowl or individual serving dishes.
6. Refrigerate at least 30 minutes (up to 3 days).

Per Serving: 170 Calories, 3g Protein, 8g Total Fat, 24g Carbohydrates, 1g Fiber, 4g Sugar, 75mg Sodium, 5mg Cholesterol

Chef Ozzie Tips

Top with Ideal®
Whipped Cream.

Challah Bread Pudding

Serves: 16

Ingredients

1 (1-pound) challah bread loaf,
    crusts trimmed and reserved, bread
    cut into $\frac{1}{2}$-inch cubes

8 large eggs

2 cups light whipping cream

2 cups 2% milk

2 cups Ideal® No Calorie Sweetener

$\frac{1}{4}$ cup hazelnut liqueur or amaretto

1 tablespoon vanilla extract

$\frac{1}{2}$ teaspoon almond extract

Directions

1. Preheat oven to 350°F.
2. Place bread cubes in 13-inch × 9-inch baking pan.
3. Whisk eggs, whipping cream, milk, Ideal®, liqueur, vanilla and almond extract in a large bowl to blend. Pour over bread cubes. Let stand 30 minutes, occasionally pressing bread into custard mixture. (Can be prepared 2 hours ahead. Cover and refrigerate.)
4. Arrange reserved bread crusts on baking sheet and bake until dry (about 10 minutes). Cool.
5. Transfer crusts to food processor and grind into fine crumbs. Sprinkle 1 cup crust crumbs over top of pudding. Bake until pudding is set in center (about 40 minutes). Cool slightly. Serve warm.

Per Serving: 270 Calories, 8g Protein, 14g Total Fat, 27g Carbohydrates, 1g Fiber, 6g Sugar, 190mg Sodium, 155mg Cholesterol

Chef Ozzie Tips

Stale bread works best in bread puddings. Simply unwrap and leave out 6 to 8 hours or overnight.

Grape-Nuts® Pudding

Serves: 8

Ingredients

1 quart 2% milk, scalded

1 cup Grape-Nuts® cereal

1 cup egg substitute

½ cup Ideal® No Calorie Sweetener

1 tablespoon pure vanilla extract

Pinch of salt

Ground nutmeg

Nonstick spray

Directions

1. Preheat oven to 350°F.
2. In a medium bowl, pour scalded milk over Grape-Nuts® and allow to soak for 5 minutes.
3. In another medium bowl, mix egg substitute, Ideal®, vanilla and salt; add egg mixture to milk/Grape-Nuts®; stir well.
4. Coat a 2-quart baking dish with nonstick spray. Pour mixture in dish. Sprinkle generous amount of nutmeg over top. Place casserole into a deep roasting pan and pour water into pan to halfway up baking dish sides. Place in oven and bake 40 to 55 minutes, until almost set in center (slight jiggle).

Per Serving: 160 Calories, 9g Protein, 3.5g Total Fat, 21g Carbohydrates, 2g Fiber, 6g Sugar, 200mg Sodium, 10mg Cholesterol

*Grape-Nuts is a registered trademark of Post Foods, LLC.

Chef Ozzie Tips

Top with Ideal® Whipped Cream.

Sweet Potato Mousse

Serves: 12

Ingredients

3 pounds whole sweet potatoes
2 pounds carrots, peeled, 1-inch pieces
$^1/_2$ cup Ideal® No Calorie Sweetener
4 tablespoons butter substitute spread

$^1/_2$ teaspoon salt
$^1/_4$ cup Ideal® Brown Sweetener
$^1/_4$ teaspoon ground cinnamon
$^1/_8$ teaspoon ground nutmeg
$^1/_4$ cup half & half

Directions

1. Preheat oven to 400°F.
2. Wash and cut ends off sweet potatoes. Place on roasting pan and bake for 50 to 60 minutes or until tender; cool slightly and peel.
3. Place peeled cut carrots in medium saucepan with straight sides; just cover carrots with water and add $^1/_2$ cup Ideal®.
4. Cook carrots on low until all liquid is gone and only syrup remains; remove from heat.
5. In a food processer, combine cooked carrots and sweet potatoes with syrup.
6. Add butter substitute, salt, Ideal® Brown, cinnamon and nutmeg and process until smooth.
7. While still processing, slowly add half & half until combined and lighter in color.
8. Spoon mixture into buttered pie dish, make fancy top with back of spoon or spatula.
9. Refrigerate until ready to use or bake at 375°F for 20 minutes or until top begins to lightly brown. Serve warm.

Per Serving: 180 Calories, 3g Protein, 3.5g Total Fat, 35g Carbohydrates, 6g Fiber, 13g Sugar, 220mg Sodium, 0mg Cholesterol

Chef Ozzie Tips

Top with mini marshmallows before baking.

Drinks
for every
Occasion

Hot Cocoa Mix

Serves: 9 to 12

Ingredients

1 cup dry nonfat milk powder
1 cup Ideal® No Calorie Sweetener

½ cup unsweetened cocoa powder
½ cup nondairy creamer
Dash salt

Directions

1. Place all ingredients in blender and process until combined.
2. Dissolve 3 to 4 tablespoons into one cup boiling water.

Per Serving: 70 Calories, 3g Protein, 1.5g Total Fat, 12g Carbohydrates, 1g Fiber, 3g Sugar, 170mg Sodium, 0mg Cholesterol

Chef Ozzie Tips

Put remaining mix in airtight container and store in a dark location for hot cocoa in an instant.

Once upon a time, money did grow on trees. Cocoa beans were used as currency by the Mayan and Aztec civilizations over 1,400 years ago. When they had too much money to spend, they brewed the excess into hot chocolate drinks.

Vanilla Milkshake

Serves: 2

Ingredients

1 pint (4 large scoops) Ideal® Vanilla Bean
    Ice Cream

½ cup 2% milk

2 tablespoons (heaping) Ideal®
    No Calorie Sweetener

1 teaspoon pure vanilla extract

Whole strawberries for garnish

Directions

1. Combine all ingredients in a blender; blend until smooth.
2. Pour in glasses and garnish with strawberry on rim.

Per Serving: 260 Calories, 8g Protein, 11g Total Fat, 34g Carbohydrates, 1g Fiber, 14g Sugar, 140mg Sodium, 75mg Cholesterol

In the early days, milkshakes did not just include the typical ingredients of milk, ice cream, and flavoring. Back then, a little whiskey was added to milkshakes.

Chef Ozzie Tips

Strawberry milkshake—mix 1 cup fresh sliced strawberries with 2 tablespoons Ideal®. Allow to rest for 20 minutes, then add to above before blending.

Mixed Berry Milkshake

Serves: 6

Ingredients

4½ cups ice cubes

3 cups 2% milk

⅓ cup Ideal® No Calorie Sweetener

2 cups frozen mixed berries

1 teaspoon pure vanilla extract

Directions

1. Combine all ingredients in blender; blend until smooth

Per Serving: 90 Calories, 4g Protein, 2.5g Total Fat, 14g Carbohydrates, 1g Fiber, 9g Sugar, 50mg Sodium, 10mg Cholesterol

Chef Ozzie Tips

Fun treat when frozen into popsicles for kids.

The first milkshake is documented in print in 1885 in a newspaper.

Strawberry Lemonade

Serves: 6

Ingredients

2 cups cold water

1 cup Ideal® No Calorie Sweetener

1 tablespoon grated lemon zest

1 cup fresh lemon juice

1 pint (12 ounces) fresh strawberries

2 cups cold sparkling water or club soda

Ice

Directions

1. In medium saucepan, bring the water and Ideal® to a boil; reduce heat and simmer, stirring occasionally until the sweetener dissolves.
2. Add lemon zest and lemon juice; stir and remove from the heat. Allow to cool completely and strain into a pitcher.
3. Purée the fresh strawberries in a blender and add to pitcher with lemon water blend. Stir well and refrigerate until chilled.
4. Add sparkling water. Stir well and serve over ice.

Per Serving: 60 Calories, 1g Protein, 0g Total Fat, 16g Carbohydrates, 1g Fiber, 4g Sugar, 0mg Sodium, 0mg Cholesterol

Chef Ozzie Tips

Garnish with fresh mint sprigs and whole strawberries.

Old-Fashioned Lemonade

Serves: 16

Ingredients

1 cup hot water
2 cups Ideal® No Calorie Sweetener
2 cups fresh or bottled lemon juice

Cold water to fill to 1 gallon pitcher
Lemon slices for garnish
Mint sprigs for garnish

Directions

1. In a small saucepan, add 1 cup water and Ideal®.
2. Bring to a boil and remove from heat, stir until completely dissolved. Chill this "simple syrup."
3. Squeeze juice from lemons. Add lemon juice to 1 gallon pitcher or container.
4. Add syrup and fill container with cold water.
5. Pour lemonade into a glass filled with ice and garnish with a lemon slice and mint sprig.

Per Serving: 35 Calories, 0g Protein, 0g Total Fat, 9g Carbohydrates, 0g Fiber, 1g Sugar, 10mg Sodium, 0mg Cholesterol

Chef Ozzie Tips

Lemons or limes at room temperature will yield more juice than when refrigerated. Microwaving the lemon or lime for a few seconds will help extract more juice.

The main types of lemons produced in the United States are the Eureka, the Lisbon, the Genoa, the Sicily, the Belair, and the Villafranca.

Citrus Breeze

Serves: 1

Ingredients

½ lemon
½ lime
½ orange

Ice cubes
1¼ cups water
4 teaspoons Ideal® No Calorie Sweetener
(or 2 packets)

Directions

1. Squeeze the juice from lemon, lime and orange; pour into large glass with ice.
2. Stir water and Ideal® into juices; mix well.
3. Garnish with fruit slices.

Per Serving: 70 Calories, 1g Protein, 0g Total Fat, 20g Carbohydrates, 4g Fiber, 8g Sugar, 10mg Sodium, 0mg Cholesterol

Chef Ozzie Tips

Use only fresh-squeezed juices for optimal flavor and benefits.

Lemon trees grow to be about 10 to 20 feet tall and are sparsely covered with foliage.

Cocoa Almond Coffee

Serves: 1

Ingredients

1 cup strong brewed coffee

2 packets Ideal® No Calorie Sweetener

2 teaspoons unsweetened cocoa powder

1/4 teaspoon almond extract

Directions

1. Combine all ingredients in coffee cup or mug; stir well and serve immediately.

Per Serving: 30 Calories, 1g Protein, 0g Total Fat, 6g Carbohydrates, 1g Fiber, 0g Sugar, 0mg Sodium, 0mg Cholesterol

Chef Ozzie Tips

Can use caffeine-free coffee.

Coffee is only grown near the equator, from the Tropic of Cancer to the Tropic of Capricorn, within a 1,000-mile limit.

Margaritas

Serves: 1

Ingredients

Margarita or kosher salt
1 jigger (1½ ounces) tequila
2 tablespoons fresh lime juice
¼ cup water

¼ teaspoon orange extract
2 tablespoons Ideal® No Calorie Sweetener
  (or 3 packets)
Ice—small handful

Directions

1. Wet rim of glass and dip into plate of salt.
2. Combine all remaining ingredients and serve over ice, strained or frozen (blended).

Per Serving: 140 Calories, 0g Protein, 0g Total Fat, 9g Carbohydrates, 0g Fiber, 1g Sugar, 480mg Sodium, 0mg Cholesterol

Chef Ozzie Tips

Flavor and color salt to match flavor profile of margarita (for example, purple salt for Pomegranate Margarita).

National margarita day is February 22nd in the United States.

Mojito

Serves: 1

Ingredients

2 tablespoons Ideal® No Calorie Sweetener
    (or 3 packets)
1 ounce (2 tablespoons) lime juice
8 mint leaves

Ice cubes
1 jigger (1½ ounces) white rum
2 ounces (4 tablespoons) club soda
1 lime wedge for garnish
1 mint sprig for garnish

Directions

1. Place Ideal®, lime juice and mint leaves into a large tumbler. Crush and combine ingredients in glass, using muddling stick or spoon, until Ideal® is dissolved.
2. Fill glass ¾ full with ice, add rum and top with club soda.

Per Serving: 130 Calories, 0g Protein, 0g Total Fat, 9g Carbohydrates, 0g Fiber, 1g Sugar, 0mg Sodium, 0mg Cholesterol

Chef Ozzie Tips

Great with muddled pomegranate seeds and juice.

Sweet Tea

Serves: 8

Ingredients

1 pinch baking soda
2 cups boiling water
6 tea bags

¾ cup Ideal® No Calorie Sweetener
(or 16 packets)
6 cups cool water

Directions

1. Sprinkle baking soda into a 64-ounce heatproof pitcher, preferably glass.
2. Pour in boiling water; add tea bags, cover and steep for 20 minutes.
3. Remove tea bags and discard; stir in Ideal® until dissolved.
4. Pour in cool water and refrigerate until cold.
5. Serve room temperature over ice with wedge of lemon.

Per Serving: 20 Calories, 0g Protein, 0g Total Fat, 4g Carbohydrates, 0g Fiber, 0g Sugar, 20mg Sodium, 0mg Cholesterol

Chef Ozzie Tips

Use caffeine-free
or your favorite
flavor of tea instead
of regular tea bags.

Fresh Mint and Citrus Tea

Serves: 10

Ingredients

2 cups boiling water
5 regular-size tea bags
1/2 cup loosely packed fresh mint leaves

1 cup Ideal® No Calorie Sweetener
6 cups water
1/3 cup fresh lemon juice
1 cup fresh orange juice

Directions

1. Pour boiling water over tea bags and mint leaves; cover and steep for 5 minutes.
2. Remove tea bags and mint; squeeze both gently.
3. Stir in Ideal® and remaining ingredients.
4. Serve over ice.

Per Serving: 35 Calories, 0g Protein, 0g Total Fat, 8g Carbohydrates, 0g Fiber, 2g Sugar, 10mg Sodium, 0mg Cholesterol

Chef Ozzie Tips

Garnish with fresh lemon and orange slices and fresh mint sprigs.

There are 30 species of mint. The two most commonly available are peppermint and spearmint.

Brunch
&
Breads

Waffles

Serves: 6

Ingredients

2 eggs
2 cups all-purpose flour
1³/₄ cups skim milk
¹/₂ cup vegetable oil

4 teaspoons baking powder
1 tablespoon Ideal® No Calorie Sweetener
   (or 1¹/₂ packets)
¹/₄ teaspoon salt
¹/₂ teaspoon pure vanilla extract

Directions

1. Preheat waffle iron.
2. Beat eggs in large bowl with mixer until fluffy.
3. Beat in flour, milk, vegetable oil, baking powder, Ideal®, salt and vanilla until smooth.
4. Pour mix onto hot waffle iron; cook until golden brown.

Per Serving: 370 Calories, 9g Protein, 21g Total Fat, 38g Carbohydrates, 1g Fiber, 3g Sugar, 520mg Sodium, 75mg Cholesterol

Chef Ozzie Tips

Serve hot with your favorite topping.

The inventor of the waffle iron did not like waffles.

Overnight French Toast

Serves: 6

Ingredients

¼ cup butter substitute spread,
    room temperature
12 (¾-inch-thick) slices French bread
1½ cups egg substitute
1½ cups 2% milk

⅓ cup Ideal® No Calorie Sweetener
1 teaspoon maple flavoring
2 tablespoons Ideal® Brown Sweetener
1 teaspoon pure vanilla extract
½ teaspoon salt

Directions

1. Cover bottom of heavy baking pan with butter substitute. Arrange bread slices in pan.
2. Beat together eggs, milk, Ideal®, maple flavor, Ideal® Brown, vanilla and salt in medium bowl. Pour mixture over bread; turn bread over once and cover with plastic. Refrigerate overnight.
3. Preheat oven to 400°F. Bake bread 10 minutes. Turn over and then continue to bake until just golden. Transfer cooked slices to plate and sprinkle with Ideal® Confectionery Sweetener; serve immediately.

Per Serving: 530 Calories, 25g Protein, 12g Total Fat, 80g Carbohydrates, 3g Fiber, 9g Sugar, 1220mg Sodium, 5mg Cholesterol

Chef Ozzie Tips

Top with your favorite fruits (slightly sweetened with Ideal®). For orange flavored toast, add ½ cup fresh-squeezed orange juice and reduce milk by ½ cup.

Sour Cream Coffee Cake

Serves: 16

Ingredients

CAKE:

1 cup (2 sticks) light, unsalted butter

1$\frac{1}{2}$ cups Ideal® No Calorie Sweetener

2 eggs

1 cup low-fat sour cream

$\frac{1}{4}$ cup milk

1 teaspoon pure vanilla

2 cups flour

1$\frac{1}{2}$ teaspoons baking powder

$\frac{1}{2}$ teaspoon baking soda

$\frac{1}{2}$ teaspoon salt

STREUSEL TOPPING:

1$\frac{1}{2}$ cups Ideal® No Calorie Sweetener

$\frac{3}{4}$ cup flour

2 teaspoons cinnamon

$\frac{1}{2}$ cup (1 stick) light, unsalted butter

SWIRL:

2 tablespoons Ideal® No Calorie Sweetener

1 tablespoon cinnamon

Directions

1. Preheat oven to 350°F.
2. Combine butter and Ideal® together until blended.
3. Add eggs, sour cream, milk and vanilla; mix.
4. Add flour, baking powder, baking soda and salt; mix.
5. For streusel, sift together 1$\frac{1}{2}$ cups Ideal®, flour and cinnamon; stir in softened butter with a fork until mixture is crumbly.
6. Grease a nonstick bundt pan; sprinkle bottom of pan with half the streusel mix.

7. Put half the batter in the pan.
8. Mix swirl ingredients and sprinkle over batter, then cover with remaining batter.
9. Sprinkle remaining streusel topping over top of cake.
10. Bake for 50 to 60 minutes or until toothpick inserted comes out clean.
11. Let cool on rack, turn over and remove from pan.

Per Serving: 260 Calories, 5g Protein, 14g Total Fat, 28g Carbohydrates, 1g Fiber, 1g Sugar, 190mg Sodium, 55mg Cholesterol

Chef Ozzie Tips

Raspberry preserves are pretty and delicious when used for the swirl.

Ozzie's Scones

Serves: 8

Ingredients

2 cups all-purpose flour

1/3 cup Ideal® No Calorie Sweetener

1 teaspoon baking powder

1/4 teaspoon baking soda

1/2 teaspoon salt

1/2 cup (1 stick) unsalted butter, frozen

1/3 cup raisins

1/2 cup sour cream

2 large eggs

1 tablespoon skim milk

Directions

1. Preheat oven to 400°F.
2. In medium bowl, mix flour, Ideal®, baking powder, baking soda and salt.
3. Grate butter into flour mixture on the large holes of grater (mixture should resemble coarse meal); add raisins.
4. In small bowl, mix sour cream and one egg until smooth.
5. Using fork, stir sour cream/egg mixture into flour mixture until large clumps form. Use hands to form ball (will be sticky at first but will come together).
6. Place on floured surface and gently roll out to thickness of 3/4 inch and approximately 8 inches in diameter.
7. Use a sharp knife and cut into 8 triangles and place on parchment-lined cookie sheet about 1 inch apart.
8. Whisk the additional egg and 1 tablespoon of milk and brush onto the tops of scones; let rest 10 minutes.

Chef Ozzie Tips

Add 1 tablespoon of fresh grated orange rind for a nice fresh flavor; flour and butter can be combined using food processor until coarse texture.

9. Bake 12 to 14 minutes until lightly golden.

10. Cool on rack or serve warm.

Per Serving: 300 Calories, 6g Protein, 15g Total Fat, 35g Carbohydrates, 1g Fiber, 7g Sugar, 280mg Sodium, 95mg Cholesterol

Cinnamon Raisin Spread

Serves: 32

Ingredients

1 1/2 cups low-fat cream cheese
1/2 cup cottage cheese, drained
1 teaspoon ground cinnamon

2 tablespoons Ideal® No Calorie Sweetener
1/2 teaspoon pure vanilla extract
1/2 cup raisins

Directions

1. Place cream cheese, cottage cheese, cinnamon, Ideal® and vanilla in food processor. Blend until smooth. Transfer to medium bowl.
2. Stir in raisins; cover and chill in refrigerator until serving.

Per Serving: 35 Calories, 1g Protein, 2g Total Fat, 3g Carbohydrates, 0g Fiber, 1g Sugar, 65mg Sodium, 5mg Cholesterol

Chef Ozzie Tips

Can add 1/4 cup chopped walnuts for added flavor.

It takes more than 4 tons of grapes to produce 1 ton of raisins.

Banana Bread

Serves: 12

Ingredients

1 cup Ideal® No Calorie Sweetener

½ cup (1 stick) butter, softened

2 eggs

1½ cups flour

1 teaspoon baking soda

1 teaspoon salt

1 cup mashed very ripe bananas

½ cup sour cream

1 teaspoon pure vanilla extract

½ cup chopped walnuts or pecans

Directions

1. Preheat oven to 350°F.
2. Butter and flour a 9-inch × 5-inch loaf pan.
3. Cream Ideal® and butter until creamy. Add eggs and beat well.
4. Sift the dry ingredients together and combine with butter mixture; blend well.
5. Add the bananas, sour cream and vanilla. Stir well.
6. Stir in nuts and pour into prepared pan.
7. Bake 1 hour or until toothpick inserted in center comes out clean. Turn onto rack and cool.

Per Serving: 220 Calories, 4g Protein, 13g Total Fat, 21g Carbohydrates, 1g Fiber, 3g Sugar, 380mg Sodium, 65mg Cholesterol

Banana plants are the largest plants on earth without a woody stem. They are actually giant herbs of the same family as lilies, orchids, and palms.

Chef Ozzie Tips

Sprinkling the batter and topping with chocolate chips before baking produces a nice dessert version.

Pumpkin Bread

Serves: 24

Ingredients

1 cup (2 sticks) margarine

3 cups Ideal® No Calorie Sweetener

3 eggs

2 teaspoons pure vanilla extract

3 cups all-purpose flour

1 tablespoon baking powder

1½ teaspoons baking soda

2 teaspoons ground cinnamon

½ teaspoon ground cloves

½ teaspoon ground nutmeg

½ teaspoon salt

Pinch of ground ginger

1 (15-ounce) can solid pack pumpkin

Directions

1. Preheat oven to 350°F.
2. In a large mixing bowl, cream margarine with Ideal®; add eggs and vanilla and mix well.
3. Combine all dry ingredients and add to creamed mixture until just moistened.
4. Stir in pumpkin and pour into two greased 9-inch × 5-inch loaf pans. Bake in oven for 50 minutes or until toothpick inserted in center comes out clean.

Per Serving: 170 Calories, 3g Protein, 8g Total Fat, 20g Carbohydrates, 1g Fiber, 1g Sugar, 280mg Sodium, 25mg Cholesterol

Chef Ozzie Tips

Add one cup golden raisins and/ or chocolate chips to batter. Sprinkle chopped nuts on top of batter before baking.

Blueberry Streusel Muffins

Serves: 12

Ingredients

MUFFIN:
1 cup Ideal® No Calorie
   Sweetener
¹/₂ cup (1 stick) unsalted
   butter, softened
2 large eggs

2 cups flour
2 teaspoons baking powder
¹/₂ teaspoon salt
¹/₂ cup milk
1 teaspoon pure vanilla extract
2 cups blueberries

STREUSEL:
¹/₄ cup Ideal® No Calorie
   Sweetener
4 tablespoons flour
1 tablespoon butter
³/₄ teaspoon cinnamon

Directions

1. Preheat oven to 375°F. Grease 12-cup muffin pan.
2. Cream Ideal® and butter until light and fluffy.
3. Add eggs one at a time, mixing well after each addition.
4. Combine flour, baking powder and salt.
5. Add alternately to butter mixture with milk and vanilla.
6. Crush ¹/₂ cup blueberries and add to batter.
7. Fold remaining blueberries into batter and spoon into muffin pan.
8. Blend all streusel ingredients with pastry blender until crumbly and sprinkle onto batter. Bake 30 minutes or until toothpick inserted in center comes out clean.
9. Cool in pan 5 minutes and turn onto wire rack.

Per Serving: 220 Calories, 4g Protein, 10g Total Fat, 28g Carbohydrates, 1g Fiber, 3g Sugar, 210mg Sodium, 60mg Cholesterol

Chef Ozzie Tips

Check your newspaper's community section for local farmers' markets to find the best fresh blueberries of the season.

Cappuccino Streusel Muffins

Serves: 8

Ingredients

STREUSEL:
1/2 cup all-purpose flour

1/4 cup Ideal® Brown
  Sweetener

1/4 teaspoon ground cinnamon

1/4 cup plus 1 teaspoon butter
  substitute spread

BATTER:
2 cups all-purpose flour

1/2 cup Ideal® No Calorie
  Sweetener

1 tablespoon baking powder

2 tablespoons instant coffee
  (if granular, crush to powder)

1 teaspoon ground cinnamon

1 cup 2% milk

2 teaspoons pure
  vanilla extract

1/4 cup egg substitute

1/2 cup vegetable oil

1/2 cup sugar-free
  chocolate chips

Directions

1. Preheat oven to 375°F. Grease cups of a muffin tin or line with paper muffin liners.
2. Combine 1/2 cup flour, Ideal® Brown and 1/4 teaspoon cinnamon in a bowl. Cut in butter substitute until mixture forms a sticky crumble; set aside.
3. In large bowl, stir together 2 cups flour, Ideal®, baking powder, instant coffee and 1 teaspoon cinnamon.
4. In a separate bowl, beat together milk, vanilla, egg substitute and oil. Add to flour mixture and stir until combined. Mix in chocolate chips. (Don't overbeat, just until combined.)
5. Spoon batter into prepared muffins pans, filling each cup all the way to the top.
6. Sprinkle streusel mixture over the top of the unbaked muffins.
7. Bake 15 minutes or until toothpick inserted near center comes out clean. Cool 5 minutes; remove to cooling rack.

Per Serving: 430 Calories, 6g Protein, 25g Total Fat, 48g Carbohydrates, 2g Fiber, 4g Sugar, 280mg Sodium, 5mg Cholesterol

Cinnamon Toast Muffins

Serves: 8

Ingredients

1½ cups all-purpose flour
¾ cup Ideal® No Calorie Sweetener
1½ teaspoons baking powder
¼ teaspoon nutmeg
⅛ teaspoon salt

¼ cup egg substitute
½ cup 2% milk
⅓ cup butter substitute spread, melted
¼ cup Ideal® No Calorie Sweetener
½ teaspoon ground cinnamon
¼ cup butter substitute spread, melted

Directions

1. Preheat oven to 350°F. Grease muffin cups or line with paper muffin liners.
2. In a medium bowl, stir together flour, ¾ cup Ideal®, baking powder, nutmeg and salt. Make a well in center of mixture; stir together egg substitute, milk and ⅓ cup melted butter substitute. Stir in egg mixture to flour mixture until just moistened; spoon batter into muffin cups.
3. Bake for 15 to 20 minutes. Meanwhile, combine ¼ cup Ideal® and cinnamon. When muffins are finished baking, immediately brush tops with ¼ cup melted butter substitute and sprinkle with Ideal®/cinnamon blend.

Per Serving: 220 Calories, 4g Protein, 11g Total Fat, 25g Carbohydrates, 1g Fiber, 1g Sugar, 260mg Sodium, 0mg Cholesterol

Chef Ozzie Tips

Enjoy with Ideal®
Cocoa Almond
Coffee.

Six-Week Muffins

Serves: 48

Ingredients

15 ounces (1 box) raisin bran cereal

2⅓ cups Ideal® No Calorie Sweetener

5 cups white whole wheat flour

5 teaspoons baking soda

2 teaspoons salt

1 cup vegetable oil

1 cup egg substitute

4 cups low-fat buttermilk

½ cup raisins

Directions

1. Preheat oven to 375°F.
2. Mix together first five ingredients.
3. Add oil, egg substitute, buttermilk and raisins; stir well.
4. Place in sealable plastic container in refrigerator until ready for use (preferably overnight).
5. When ready to bake, scoop into greased muffin pans. Fill any unused wells with small amount of water. If batter becomes too stiff, stir in 2% milk, buttermilk or melted butter substitute until desired consistency is achieved.
6. Batter will keep for 6 weeks in a closed container in refrigerator.
7. Bake 15 to 20 minutes until golden brown.

Per Serving: 140 Calories, 4g Protein, 6g Total Fat, 20g Carbohydrates, 3g Fiber, 4g Sugar, 300mg Sodium, 0mg Cholesterol

Chef Ozzie Tips

Add a small amount of any of the following for a new flavor: dried fruits, pecans, walnuts, oats, wheat germ, flax seed, cinnamon, Grape Nuts®, chopped apples, or bananas.

Raspberry Lemon Muffins

Serves: 8

Ingredients

½ cup plain low-fat yogurt

3 tablespoons vegetable oil

1 tablespoon fresh lemon juice

2 egg whites

1 teaspoon lemon extract

1½ cups all-purpose flour

1¼ cups Ideal® No Calorie Sweetener

2 teaspoons baking powder

¼ teaspoon salt

1 teaspoon lemon zest

1 cup frozen raspberries

1 tablespoon butter substitute spread

1 tablespoon Ideal® No Calorie Sweetener

Chef Ozzie Tips

Substitute canola oil for vegetable oil for a healthier option.

Directions

1. Preheat oven to 400°F. Grease muffin tin or line with paper muffin liners (spray papers as well).
2. In large bowl, mix together yogurt, oil, lemon juice, egg whites and lemon extract.
3. In separate bowl, stir together flour, 1¼ cups Ideal®, baking powder, salt and lemon zest.
4. Add the wet ingredients to the dry mix and combine completely. Gently stir in frozen raspberries.
5. Spoon batter evenly into the prepared muffin cups. Bake for 12 to 14 minutes or until the top springs back when lightly pressed; cool muffins (still in tin) on a wire rack. Just out of the oven, melt 1 tablespoon butter substitute and brush on warm muffins; sprinkle with 1 tablespoon Ideal®.

Per Serving: 200 Calories, 4g Protein, 7g Total Fat, 29g Carbohydrates, 1g Fiber, 2g Sugar, 250mg Sodium, 0mg Cholesterol

Banana Coconut Muffins

Serves: 10

Ingredients

1¼ cups all-purpose flour
1 teaspoon baking powder
¼ teaspoon salt
3 very ripe bananas, mashed

1 teaspoon pure vanilla extract
½ cup (1 stick) unsalted butter, melted
⅔ cup Ideal® No Calorie Sweetener
1 large egg
¾ cup sweetened flaked coconut

Directions

1. Preheat oven to 375°F. Position oven rack in middle of oven. Line muffin tin with paper liners.
2. Whisk together flour, baking powder and salt in a bowl.
3. Mix together bananas, vanilla, butter, Ideal®, egg and ½ cup coconut in large bowl until well combined.
4. Fold in flour mixture until flour is just moistened.
5. Divide among lined muffin cups. Sprinkle with remaining ¼ cup of coconut and gently press into batter.
6. Bake until muffins are puffed and golden (about 20 minutes).
7. Transfer to rack and cool.

Per Serving: 180 Calories, 3g Protein, 9g Total Fat, 23g Carbohydrates, 1g Fiber, 3g Sugar, 125mg Sodium, 35mg Cholesterol

There are more than 500 varieties of bananas in the world.

Chef Ozzie Tips

Bananas freeze well—the peel will brown but the inside will stay delicious. Simply allow to thaw before mashing to use in a recipe.

Savory
Dishes

Noni's Teriyaki Wings

Serves: 8

Ingredients

5 ounces (½ bottle) low-sodium soy sauce
1 cup Ideal® Brown Sweetener

3 cloves fresh garlic, sliced thin
4 pounds frozen or raw chicken wings

Directions

1. Mix together soy sauce, Ideal® Brown and garlic.
2. Toss mixture with wings and place in large zip-lock bag; refrigerate overnight.
3. Pour wings and marinade in large stockpot. Bring to a boil and simmer for 15 minutes.
4. Pour wings and marinade in shallow baking pan with 1-inch sides. Bake in a 425°F oven for 20 to 25 minutes or until nicely browned.

Per Serving: 560 Calories, 43g Protein, 36g Total Fat, 13g Carbohydrates, 0g Fiber, 12g Sugar, 560mg Sodium, 170mg Cholesterol

Chef Ozzie Tips

Garlic heads and cloves should not be stored in your refrigerator. If garlic is refrigerated, it is likely to get soft and moldy.

Approximately 90 percent of the garlic grown in the United States is grown in California.

Chicken Marsala

Serves: 6

Ingredients

½ cup all-purpose flour

1 teaspoon fine sea salt

½ teaspoon black pepper

3 (7-ounce) chicken breasts, sliced in halves and pounded thin and even

4 tablespoons olive oil

4 tablespoons unsalted butter

2 cups fresh mushrooms, sliced (shiitake, button, white)

½ cup marsala wine

2 cups chicken stock

3 teaspoons Ideal® No Calorie Sweetener

¼ cup half & half

Fine sea salt (to taste)

Fresh ground pepper (to taste)

Directions

1. Combine flour, 1 teaspoon sea salt and ½ teaspoon pepper. Cover chicken pieces in flour mixture and shake off excess.

2. Heat 2 tablespsoons oil in large skillet on medium heat until hot but not smoking. Add 1 tablespoon butter and sauté chicken until golden brown on both sides. Add 2 tablespoons olive oil to pan with 1 tablespoon butter and sauté mushrooms; cook until just slightly brown. Add marsala and bring to a boil, scraping pan to remove any bits from bottom of pan. When wine is reduced by half, add chicken stock; simmer for 5 minutes. Add Ideal® and half & half and cook for 10 minutes.

3. Lower heat to simmer and add chicken back to pan; simmer an additional 10 minutes until chicken is fully cooked. Swirl in 2 tablespoons butter. Season with salt and pepper to taste. Transfer chicken to large platter; top with sauce.

Per Serving: 530 Calories, 19g Protein, 35g Total Fat, 31g Carbohydrates, 2g Fiber, 4g Sugar, 1010mg Sodium, 65mg Cholesterol

Chef Ozzie Tips

Garnish with chopped scallions and fresh parsley.

Shrimp Linguini with Lemon Oil

Serves: 4

Ingredients

LEMON OIL:
1/2 cup extra-virgin olive oil
1 lemon, zested

PASTA:
16 ounces linguini
2 tablespoons extra-virgin
    olive oil

2 shallots, diced
2 large garlic cloves, minced
16 ounces medium
    frozen shrimp
1/4 cup fresh-squeezed lemon
    juice (about 2 lemons)
1 lemon, zested
2 packets Ideal® No Calorie
    Sweetener

1 teaspoon ground sea salt
1/2 teaspoon fresh ground
    black pepper
3 ounces arugula
    (about 3 packed cups)
1/4 cup chopped fresh parsley

Directions

1. Combine olive oil and lemon zest in small bowl and set aside for 20 to 30 minutes.
2. Bring large pot of salted water to a boil. Add pasta and cook until tender but still "al dente" (firm to the bite)—about 8 to 10 minutes.
3. Drain pasta and reserve 1 cup pasta water.
4. In a large skillet, heat olive oil over medium heat; add shallots and garlic and cook for 2 minutes; add shrimp and cook until pink (about 5 minutes). Add cooked linguini, lemon juice, lemon zest, Ideal®, salt and pepper. Toss to combine.
5. Add arugula, pasta water and strained lemon oil (discard zest).
6. Add chopped parsley; toss and serve immediately.

Per Serving: 890 Calories, 40g Protein, 39g Total Fat, 95g Carbohydrates, 5g Fiber, 6g Sugar, 770mg Sodium, 170mg Cholesterol

Top with fresh grated
Parmesan cheese.
Using whole wheat
pasta provides
more fiber.

Tomato Sauce

Serves: 16

Ingredients

½ cup extra-virgin olive oil

2 large Spanish onions

8 medium garlic cloves, peeled and sliced thin

2 tablespoons dry thyme leaves, chopped

1 medium carrot, peeled and finely diced

4 (28-ounce) cans whole peeled tomatoes, hand crushed in juice

2 tablespoons Ideal® No Calorie Sweetener

Salt

Directions

1. In large saucepan, heat olive oil over medium heat, add onions and garlic and cook until just tender and light brown.
2. Add thyme and carrot and cook an additional 5 minutes until carrots are soft. Add tomatoes with juice and bring to boil, stirring frequently.
3. Lower heat to simmer and cook for 40 minutes until thick. Add Ideal® and season with salt.

Per Serving: 100 Calories, 2g Protein, 7g Total Fat, 9g Carbohydrates, 2g Fiber, 5g Sugar, 300mg Sodium, 0mg Cholesterol

Olive oil is a natural juice which preserves the taste, aroma, and vitamins of the olive fruit. Olive oil offers protection against heart disease by controlling LDL "bad" cholesterol levels while raising HDL "good" cholesterol levels.

Chef Ozzie Tips

The more you crush or smash garlic, the more essential oils will be released. For milder garlic flavor, slice instead of crushing.

Italian Chopped Salad

Serves: 4

Ingredients

2 tablespoons fresh lemon juice
2 teaspoons Ideal® No Calorie Sweetener
1 small garlic clove, minced
1 small shallot, minced
1/2 teaspoon ground sea salt
1/4 teaspoon fresh ground black pepper
1/2 cup extra-virgin olive oil

3 cups chopped romaine
1/2 cup chopped radicchio
1 English cucumber, diced
2 medium tomatoes, diced
1 yellow pepper, diced
1 small red onion, diced
1 cup fresh flat-leaf parsley leaves
1/2 cup black olives, quartered

Directions

1. Whisk together lemon juice, Ideal®, garlic, shallot, salt and pepper.
2. Add olive oil in slow steady stream whisking constantly until combined.
3. Combine remaining ingredients and toss with dressing.

Per Serving: 350 Calories, 3g Protein, 30g Total Fat, 17g Carbohydrates, 4g Fiber, 7g Sugar, 460mg Sodium, 0mg Cholesterol

Chef Ozzie Tips

Substitute balsamic vinegar for lemon juice, or add iceberg lettuce.

100% natural sea salt maintains integrity. All of the trace and micro-nutrients are fully intact, and the correct balance of sodium and chloride are present as well as calcium, magnesium, potassium, and 90 other trace and micro-nutrients.

Basil Parmesan Balsamic Dressing

Serves: 6

Ingredients

1 large garlic clove

$\frac{1}{2}$ teaspoon sea salt

2 tablespoons balsamic vinegar

1 teaspoon fresh lemon juice

2 packets Ideal® No Calorie Sweetener

3 tablespoons minced fresh basil

$\frac{1}{4}$ cup Parmesan, finely grated

$\frac{1}{4}$ teaspoon fresh cracked black pepper

$\frac{1}{2}$ cup extra-virgin olive oil

Directions

1. Mince garlic and mash to a paste with sea salt; whisk in vinegar, lemon juice, Ideal®, basil, Parmesan and pepper.
2. Add oil in slow, steady stream, whisking constantly until well blended.

Per Serving: 200 Calories, 1g Protein, 20g Total Fat, 2g Carbohydrates, 0g Fiber, 1g Sugar, 270mg Sodium, 5mg Cholesterol

Chef Ozzie Tips

Enjoy on your favorite salad.

Pepper was so valuable that in ancient Greece and Rome it was used as currency.

Coleslaw Dressing

Serves: 8

Ingredients

¾ cup mayonnaise

3 tablespoons Ideal® No Calorie Sweetener

1½ tablespoons cider vinegar

⅓ cup canola oil

⅛ teaspoon mustard, dry

⅛ teaspoon celery seed

Pinch black pepper

1 tablespoon fresh lemon juice

½ cup half & half

Pinch salt

Directions

1. In medium bowl, mix all ingredients together until well blended.
2. Cover and refrigerate.
3. Mix with bagged coleslaw cabbage mix (or chop cabbage and carrots from scratch).
4. Keep bowl covered with damp cloth until ready to use.

Per Serving: 260 Calories, 0g Protein, 28g Total Fat, 2g Carbohydrates, 0g Fiber, 0g Sugar, 135mg Sodium, 15mg Cholesterol

Chef Ozzie Tips

Use flavored vinegars, lime juice, or any dry seasonings desired for updated flavor profiles.

the
Kitchen
Sink

Texas BBQ Rub

Serves: 60 tablespoons

Ingredients

1 (16-ounce) bottle low-sodium seasoning salt
¼ cup paprika
⅔ cup chili powder
1 teaspoon ground ginger
1 teaspoon ground nutmeg

2 teaspoons ground mustard
1 teaspoon ground cloves
1 teaspoon dry mesquite-flavored seasoning mix
2 tablespoons garlic powder
1 tablespoon black pepper
1 cup Ideal® Brown Sweetener

Directions

1. In a large bowl, combine all ingredients and mix well.
2. Store in airtight container.

Per Serving: 10 Calories, 0g Protein, 0g Total Fat, 2g Carbohydrates, 0g Fiber, 2g Sugar, 2400mg Sodium, 0mg Cholesterol

Chef Ozzie Tips

Rub both sides of ribs for the best flavor.

Barbecues have been a White House tradition since Thomas Jefferson.

The Oz's Marinade

Serves: 8

Ingredients

1 cup Italian vinaigrette dressing

3 cloves fresh garlic, sliced thin

1/4 cup balsamic dressing

1/4 cup low-sodium soy sauce

3 tablespoons Ideal® Brown Sweetener

Sea salt (to taste)

Fresh ground black pepper (to taste)

Directions

1. Combine all ingredients and store in airtight container.

2. Refrigerate for up to one week.

Per Serving: 80 Calories, 1g Protein, 6g Total Fat, 8g Carbohydrates, 0g Fiber, 5g Sugar, 710mg Sodium, 0mg Cholesterol

Chef Ozzie Tips

Works well with steaks, chicken, shrimp, and roasted vegetables.

Ideal-Coated Spanish Peanuts

Serves: 21

Ingredients

1½ cups Ideal® No Calorie Sweetener

¾ cup water

1 tablespoon maple flavoring

4½ cups Spanish peanuts with skins

½ teaspoon salt

Directions

1. Preheat oven to 350°F.
2. In a large saucepan, combine the first four ingredients. Stir while cooking over medium heat for 20 minutes or until almost all the liquid is gone. Spread into a greased 15-inch × 10-inch baking pan with low sides; sprinkle with salt.
3. Place in oven for 22 to 25 minutes or until nuts are well coated; stir several times. Remove to a parchment-lined tray and cool completely.
4. Store in airtight container.

Per Serving: 190 Calories, 8g Protein, 16g Total Fat, 9g Carbohydrates, 3g Fiber, 0g Sugar, 65mg Sodium, 0mg Cholesterol

Chef Ozzie Tips

Serve over Ideal® Vanilla Bean Ice Cream and top with Ideal® Whipped Cream.

The peanut is not a nut, but a legume related to beans and lentils.

Roasted Cinnamon Almonds

Serves: 8

Ingredients

1 large egg white

1 teaspoon cold water

2 cups whole raw almonds

¾ cup Ideal® No Calorie Sweetener

¼ teaspoon salt

1½ teaspoons ground cinnamon

½ cup Ideal® No Calorie Sweetener

2 teaspoons ground cinnamon

Directions

1. Preheat oven to 250°F.
2. Lightly grease a short-sided cookie pan (10-inch × 15-inch jelly roll pan).
3. Lightly beat egg white; add water and beat until frothy but not stiff.
4. Add nuts and toss until evenly coated.
5. Mix ¾ cup Ideal®, salt and 1½ teaspoons cinnamon and toss in nut/egg white mixture until evenly coated.
6. Spread evenly on prepared pan.
7. Bake for one hour, stirring occasionally.
8. Remove from oven; leave in pan and allow to cool for 30 minutes.
9. While still sticky and warm, mix ½ cup Ideal® and 2 teaspoons cinnamon and toss with nuts, making sure to separate and coat all nuts.
10. When cool, store in airtight container.

Per Serving: 240 Calories, 8g Protein, 18g Total Fat, 16g Carbohydrates, 5g Fiber, 1g Sugar, 80mg Sodium, 0mg Cholesterol

Chef Ozzie Tips

If stored in the freezer, almonds can stay fresh for over a year.

Dessert Nachos

Serves: 6

Ingredients

3 (8- to 10-inch) whole wheat flour tortillas

Nonstick spray

$1/4$ cup water

1 tablespoon pure vanilla extract

3 tablespoons Ideal® No Calorie Sweetener

$1/2$ teaspoon ground cinnamon

2 tablespoons Ideal® No Calorie Sweetener

$3/4$ cup fat-free sour cream

$3/4$ cup frozen sugar-free whipped topping, thawed

1 teaspoon pure vanilla extract

$1/2$ teaspoon ground cinnamon

3 cups fresh fruit and berries (kiwi, strawberries, mango, blueberries, raspberries)

2 tablespoons sliced almonds, toasted

Directions

1. Preheat oven to 400°F .
2. Spray both sides of tortillas with nonstick spray.
3. Combine $1/4$ cup water and 1 tablespoon vanilla.
4. Combine 3 tablespoons Ideal® and $1/2$ teaspoon cinnamon.
5. Brush each side of tortillas with water/vanilla mixture.
6. Sprinkle each side with cinnamon and Ideal® mixture.
7. Place pieces onto wire rack on a pan.
8. Bake in oven for 8 to 10 minutes or until lightly browned; let cool.
9. In small bowl, combine 2 tablespoons Ideal®, sour cream, whipped topping, 1 teaspoon vanilla and $1/2$ teaspoon cinnamon; cover and chill.

Chef Ozzie Tips

Grated sugar-free chocolate can be added to topping.

10. Place tortillas on dessert plates, top with whipped topping mixture, fresh fruit and toasted almonds.

Per Serving: 170 Calories, 5g Protein, 3.5g Total Fat, 27g Carbohydrates, 5g Fiber, 7g Sugar, 115mg Sodium, 10mg Cholesterol
**Nutritionals based on using 1 cup strawberries, 1 cup raspberries, and 1 cup blackberries

Noodle Kugel

Serves: 8

Ingredients

Butter for dish/nonstick vegetable spray
16 ounces whole wheat pasta
1¼ cup (2½ sticks) light butter
6 ounces low-fat cream cheese
¾ cup Ideal® No Calorie Sweetener

1¼ cups egg substitute
1 teaspoon pure vanilla extract
1 cup low-fat sour cream
½ cup low-fat cottage cheese

Directions

1. Preheat oven to 350°F and butter 13-inch × 9-inch baking dish.
2. In a large pot of boiling salted water, add pasta and cook according to package directions. Drain and rinse with cold water. Place in large mixing bowl.
3. In a medium bowl, cream butter and cream cheese; mix in Ideal®, egg substitute, vanilla, sour cream and cottage cheese. Combine well.
4. Add mixture to noodles in bowl, combine well. Pour into buttered dish.
5. Bake for 45 to 60 minutes or until set and lightly browned.
6. Let rest for 15 minutes, cut into squares and serve warm or at room temperature.

Per Serving: 390 Calories, 14g Protein, 27g Total Fat, 24g Carbohydrates, 2g Fiber, 4g Sugar, 260mg Sodium, 60mg Cholesterol

Chef Ozzie Tips

Combine 1 cup cornflakes, ½ cup Ideal® Brown Sweetener and 1 teaspoon ground cinnamon; mix well and top Kugel before baking.

Whipped Cream

Serves: 16

Ingredients

2 cups good-quality heavy cream, very cold

¼ cup Ideal® No Calorie Sweetener
1 tablespoon pure vanilla extract

Directions

1. Add cold cream to large bowl and whip until peaks begin to form and cream is slightly thickened.
2. Add Ideal® and vanilla and continue whipping until stiff peaks form. Do not whip beyond stiff stage as cream will curdle. Keep in refrigerator up to 24 hours.

Per Serving: 110 Calories, 1g Protein, 11g Total Fat, 2g Carbohydrates, 0g Fiber, 0g Sugar, 10mg Sodium, 40mg Cholesterol

Chef Ozzie Tips

Try flavoring with any of the following: liqueurs, fruit or nut extracts, spices (cinnamon, pumpkin), herbs, citrus zests, ground fruits, jams, or jellies.

Healthy Sweet Benefits of Xylitol

Xylitol (zy-li-tall)

Discovered in 1891 by German chemist Emil Fischer, xylitol has been used as a sweetening agent in human food since the 1960s. Xylitol is a white crystalline powder that is odorless, with a pleasant, sweet taste. It is gaining increasing acceptance as an alternative sweetener due to its role in reducing the development of dental cavities.

Xylitol occurs naturally in many fruits and vegetables and is even produced by the human body during normal metabolism. Produced commercially from plants such as birch and other hardwood trees and fibrous vegetation, xylitol has the same sweetness and bulk as sucrose with one-third fewer calories and no unpleasant aftertaste. It quickly dissolves and produces a cooling sensation in the mouth.

Xylitol is currently approved for use in foods, pharmaceuticals, and oral health products in more than 35 countries. Xylitol is used in foods such as chewing gum, gum drops, and hard candy, and in pharmaceutical and oral health products such as throat lozenges, cough syrups, children's chewable multivitamins, toothpastes, and mouthwashes.

- Reduces new caries (cavity) formation
- Reduces plaque growth
- Stimulates salivary flow
- Safe for people with diabetes
- Safe for pregnant/nursing women
- Safe for children

Diabetes and xylitol

Control of blood glucose, lipids, and weight are the three major goals of diabetes management today. Xylitol is slowly absorbed and has a low glycemic index around 7. Therefore, when xylitol is used, the rise in blood glucose and insulin response associated with the ingestion of glucose are significantly reduced. The reduced caloric value of xylitol is consistent with the objective of weight control as well.

Dental benefits

Xylitol has been used since the mid-1970s in mainly sugar-free gums. Research confirms a plaque-reducing effect from xylitol and suggests that the compound, having some chemical properties similar to sucrose, attracts and then starves harmful micro-organisms, allowing the mouth to remineralize damaged teeth with less interruption.

Index

To order additional copies of

Sweet Revolution
COOKING WITHOUT SUGAR

contact

Heartland Sweeteners
14300 Clay Terrace Boulevard, Suite 249
Carmel, Indiana 46032

www.chefozzie.com
www.idealsweet.com
Also available on Amazon.com